Yewande Erinle

Holy Spirit Diaries

Diligent Waitress - Hadassah's Story

Copyright © 2010 Yewande Erinle
All rights reserved.

ISBN: 1-4536-3053-8
ISBN-13: 9781453630532

DEDICATION

This book is dedicated to all The King's girls; all mothers, daughters and sisters whose eyes are fixed on our Lord Jesus. To the women of substance who love the Lord with all their hearts, minds and souls. I'd also like to dedicate this book to those of you who don't know Jesus; taste and see that the Lord is good. May you all fulfil divine destiny in Jesus' name.

Forward

Yewande has captured a 'down load from heaven' in this book. It is great to see Yewande setting an example for us all and obeying Gods call on her life. She has been a hidden treasure. This book is a great reminder of the importance of relying on the Holy Spirit and obeying promptings. It will also encourage you (especially teenagers) to be bold and do things Gods way. It is a great reminder that God really does have a plan for our lives and a great one at that! I also pray it speaks to those that have been hurt in the past and unable to understand how a loving God can allow this to happen. It has reminded me of the urgent need for intercessory prayer! I believe this book will speak to those waiting on God for a Husband or Wife and also those who are currently married about the wonderful gift God has given us and the power of forgiveness.

I am already looking forward to the next sequel!

Pastor Helen Reed, Salvation for the Nations.

Acknowledgements

I must first give honour to whom honour is due, and God deserves all the honour, glory and adoration. Without Him, this would not be possible. He wrote this book and He chose to bless me by making me an instrument of His love and glory. Praise be to God.

I also want to say a big thank you to my husband for his love and support during this and other projects. Thank you to my mum for her endless prayers that are a monument before God. Thank you to my lovely children, Anu, Seyi and Fifi for your support and prayers. To my brothers and sisters; thank you all.

Thank you to my church family (Herts International Church—Salvation for the Nations) for their support; Pastors Brad and Wyona, you both are pillars of our society, a source of encouragement and wisdom and an inspiration to us all, both as leaders and as a married couple. Pastor Helen Reed, thank you so much for your support and for writing the forward for this book, God bless you. Mary Hughes, thank you for your inspiring words and loving hugs.

To all my friends, thank you for your love and support, but most especially for your friendship; I really appreciate you and God bless you all. My mum in the Lord, Pastor Freda Ajumobi;

only God can reward you, for continually labouring over your sons and daughters until Christ is formed in them.

If anyone were to ask me to pin point the origin of my walk with God, I would say that my relationship with God moved to another level during my time at the Fountain of Life Church in Welwyn garden City, Hertfordshire, UK. Pastors Kunle and Kofo Adetola; you have been very instrumental in my ever increasing walk with the Lord and although I didn't know it at the time, I do now. May God bless and increase you both.

Last and by no means least; thank you to all the readers, may this book serve as an instrument of God's wisdom for such a time as this.

Reviews

Dear Yewande,

Thank you for letting me read this first copy of your book. It's a beautiful story, written with direction of the Holy Spirit.

Mary Hughes.

This is a wonderful illustration of the way that Abba Father works in our lives. How He is interested and wants to be involved in everything we do. Anything that is important to us is important to Him. Your work shows that He is not only a relational God but constantly moves in power to intervene in our lives when we ask Him to. You have shown Him very well to be the Potter who lovingly moulds and develops us into the person He created us to be.

Dr. Brad Norman, Senior Pastor—SFTN.

It has reminded me the importance of relying on the Holy Spirit and being obedient to his promptings. I really pray this encourages other people (especially teenagers) to be bold and do things Gods way. He really does have a plan for our lives and a great one at that! I also pray it speaks to those that have been hurt in the past and unable to understand how a loving God can allow this to happen. It has reminded me of the urgent need for intercessory prayer! I also believe this will speak to those who are married about the wonderful gift God has given us.

    Pastor Helen Reed, SFTN.

Contents

Chapter 1.	Breakfast!	1
Chapter 2.	In the Beginning	5
Chapter 3.	School Days	11
Chapter 4.	Why Lord?	19
Chapter 5.	Healing	23
Chapter 6.	Uncle John	31
Chapter 7.	That Time of the Year	35
Chapter 8.	Surprise!	37
Chapter 9.	Graduation	43
Chapter 10.	Anniversary	45
Chapter 11.	A Miracle—The Power of Prayer	49
Chapter 12.	Goliath	53
Chapter 13.	Home Sweet Home	63
Chapter 14.	My Heritage	67
Chapter 15.	Bone of my Bones, Flesh of My Flesh	77
Chapter 16.	The Vows	81
Page 66	Notes	85
Page 69	Letter from 'The Father' to His Daughter	89 91
Page 72	About the author	93

Introduction

The Lord is looking for men and women who will wait on Him, just like a waiter would on you. He wants us to wait on Him always with our trays filled with praise and worship for Him. As you approach Him with your tray, He begins to take in the sweet aroma of what's on it and He comes down for a better view of what you have chosen to serve Him with. He delights in what's on your tray and more importantly, He loves it when you wait for Him to finish enjoying His meal. He wants to hear you ask Him for His needs and He wants you to keep Him company too. God has desires too, He longs for a deeper relationship with you. Your relationship with Him means much more to Him than anything else, after all this is why He sent His only son to die for us. He longs to sit and chat with you and He longs to show the world His love through you. I pray that God's love ministers to you as you read this book and that His love for you is more real to you than ever before. I pray that His love causes you to desire more of Him and to long for Him like King David did in the book of psalms. I pray that you know what it means for your soul to pant for Him. I pray that you grab hold of Him afresh and that you never let go. I pray that as you read this book, your heart becomes open to a new level of intimacy with Him and that there will be no turning back for you, just going further and deeper in His love till He comes to take us home.I pray that others will see His love in you and through you, and that they will see how much it has changed your life and your home, and they will desire it as well.

We all have our own pre-conceived ideas or expectations of what love is and how it should be expressed, and sometimes we end up getting disappointed when those who say they love us do not express their love for us the way we expect. Our own idea of love, sometimes does not meet our expectation and we think love has let us down. I want to let you know today that God is love and so He alone knows what love is and how to express it and He can never let you down. He loved you enough to lay down His life for you, so try Him today, He will fill you up with His love, give you the right definition of love and He will meet and exceed every Godly expectation you have of Him.

Chapter 1
Breakfast!

It was a lovely summer's day and I had an eleven o'clock meeting with Daren, my publisher, that morning. After my usual morning activities, which includes my prayers and some sit ups; let's face it, after three children the tummy begins to have a mind of its own. The love handles are no longer just that, if I'm not careful, sooner or later, my husband will be able to use them to lift me off the bed.

I dashed out of the kitchen and into the garage where I had the usual five minutes rummage through my bag looking for the car keys. I finally found them and it was off to the publishers. About ten minutes into my journey, I heard a rumbling noise, it was my stomach. I was in so much of a hurry that I skipped breakfast. *Great!* I thought, *my first meeting with a new publisher and all he'll be listening to is 'tunes from Dami's stomach'. This won't do, I better stop somewhere for breakfast.* I looked around and there on Fleet Street was a cosy breakfast shop. There were no parking spaces left nearby, so I had to go round the one-way system a few times hoping someone would pull out. After a few frustrating minutes of trying to find a parking space, I gave up and decided to do what I should have done first hand; I decided to call in a favour from my friend, if anyone can get me a parking space on time, He can. I really should have asked Him first instead of wasting time going round and round in circles.

Yewande Erinle

So I asked the Holy Spirit to get me the perfect parking space. Two minutes after I had asked H.S., as I like to call Him, a red Volvo pulled out from the space right in front of the breakfast shop. *Thank you Lord!* I exclaimed, *you're the best.* I pulled in and scurried to the door. This will be really quick I thought and just as I was about to step into the shop, a lovely waitress walked over to me and said, "Sorry, you're late, we're closed for the morning. We open again for lunch at 11.30." I thought to myself, *it's only 9.30am for goodness' sake, what are you doing closing up now?* I was just too hungry to give up that easily, so I moved a little closer to her and said, "Listen, do you hear that?"

"What?" she asked inquisitively.

"That!" I whispered, 'the sound of my stomach. If you don't feed me now, whatever is in there making those noises will be out to get us and God help us both if that happens." She looked at me in terror; but when she saw the smile creep onto my face, she laughed hysterically and said politely, "You're funny; OK, I can make you something real quick. Take a seat and look through the menu, and let me know what you'd like to eat."

It was quite nice being the only one in the shop that morning, I had the attention of the waitress all to myself and I felt like royalty. It made me think of how God feels when we give Him our full attention, no distractions, just Him and us.

I placed my order and waited patiently for her to get it. She came out a few minutes later to tidy up the place; I guess they had to prepare for lunch. She was humming this beautiful tune while she worked and it caught my attention.

Now there's a tune you don't hear every day, especially in a breakfast shop like this one, I thought to myself. *In fact, that's a tune I only hear at church or on my iPod.* I walked over to her quietly and hummed along with her, she looked up and smiled, and we both broke into song, "Oh! How I love Jesus, oh! How I love Jesus, oh! How I love Jesus, because He first loved me."

"What a beautiful voice you have," I said. "Are you sure you've got the right job?"

"Ooh! I have," she said. "This voice belongs to God and I sing for Him in church and everywhere else I could possible sing, but I never use it to earn a living." *How strange* I thought.

"But why?" I asked. "God has given you such a lovely gift and He did say your gift will make room for you and take you before kings, this to me means you should expect some sort of reward for it! You could be a gospel singer, I'm guessing you are a Christian, because you don't see people dedicating anything to God these days, I mean honestly speaking it takes a Godly person to think of God this way."

"I know what you mean," she replied. "Let me tell you my story and you might understand why this gift belongs exclusively to God. I really feel led to share this with you while you wait, have you got time?"

"Yes," I replied. "I have a meeting with my publisher for eleven o'clock and he's only fifteen minutes away from your restaurant."

Chapter 2
In the Beginning

"My grandparents were Jewish, they came over to the United Kingdom from Israel to make a living and build a home. After 10 years of hard work in this country, they finally bought themselves a nice house. They had two children, a boy and a girl. Their daughter, my mum, was 13 years old and her brother, my uncle, was 16 years old when a fire broke out one night after everyone had gone to bed. It was an electrical fire and the flames moved quickly through the house, my mum was in her bedroom on the second floor while my grandparents where on the first. A neighbour saw the flames and called the fire fighters, but the flames had engulfed the first floor by the time they arrived. My mother heard the commotion in her sleep; she got up and went to her window. When she realised what was happening, she started to scream for help, but she couldn't open her window and she collapsed after a few minutes. She woke up to find herself in the hospital the next day. Uncle John stayed by her side all through the night; he wasn't at home that night, he was working the night shift at the community hospital where he was studying to become a nurse. When Mum woke up, she knew something bad had happened, she asked Uncle John where their parents were, but he could not speak. He was in tears and Mum realised they had died in that fire.

"Mum was not the same again for years; she was so unhappy and very angry until she met my dad. Mum said my dad was her knight in shining armour and he was, literally; because he was one of the fire fighters who saved her life that night. He had visited her a few times in hospital after the fire and, a couple of years later; they had met up again at the village and became very good friends. Dad did not only save Mum from the fire, he also saved her from herself as she was spiralling into pit of depression. Dad was a born-again Christian and so he prayed with Mum every chance he got. They dated for a while and Dad eventually led Mum to Christ. They married a few years later.

"Mum always said that God was good to her and her brother, Uncle John; she said God sent Hosea, my father to be a father to them both. She said Dad was the next best thing that ever happened to her, Jesus was the best you see. She laughed each time she said that, because it was Dad who introduced her to Jesus.

"Mum studied medicine and got a job in America, so she and Dad decided to move there while Uncle John remained in the UK. It was hard at first for Mum to leave her brother behind, it was like a piece of her heart was being left behind, but she soon got over it. Dad found a job in a fire station not far from where they lived and things could only get better. Two years after they moved to America, Mum had twins, a boy and a girl, and she named them after her parents; Hadassah and Samuel. Oh! Excuse me for not introducing myself, I'm Dassah, my friends like to call me Esther, but I prefer Dassah," the waitress quipped.

I laughed as I replied, "Pleased to meet you; I'm Dami."

Holy Spirit Diaries

"Dami! Where's that from?"

"It's Nigerian and it's an abbreviated version of my really long name, which I'll tell you later. Right now, I'd really like to listen to your story."

"Sam and I grew up in a very happy home, we enjoyed our childhood. Dad was very strict and very loving. As for Mum; well, let's just say we learnt how to pray at an early age. It was Mum who introduced Sam and me to the Holy Spirit. You see, Sam and I gave our lives to Christ when we were seven years old and, a few weeks later, Mum began to teach us about the Holy Spirit and how it was important to be filled and led by Him. Sam and I wanted to know this Holy Spirit so we asked Mum if she could pray for us to be filled with the Holy Spirit, and she did. Sam started to speak in tongues immediately, that same hour Mum prayed, but I didn't and I wondered why.

"I was a little disappointed that I couldn't speak in tongues immediately, but never gave up bugging God about it. Mum said that not speaking in tongues doesn't mean I wasn't filled with the Holy Spirit, she said, 'Just have faith Dassah, when God is ready, He'll give you utterance.' Although I didn't know what the word 'utterance' meant, I added it to my prayer request and I said, 'Holy Spirit, the day you decide to let me speak in tongues like you did Sam, could you please tell me the meaning of the word 'utterance' too?'

"Two weeks later; just after church one Sunday morning, I was up in my room reading Acts, chapter two (I read that scripture at least once a week, I knew verses two and three by heart); I heard the words 'open your mouth and speak'. At first I was scared, I wondered who said that, I looked to see if Sam was around trying to trick me, but I was the only one upstairs. I heard the words about three times and I decided to obey. As soon as I opened up my mouth, I burst out in tongues and guess what? I got the meaning of the word 'utterance'; I kept on repeating the words, 'utterance—to speak'. I was elated, I ran downstairs shouting and singing in tongues, I could not say anything else in English apart from the words 'utterance—to speak', if I had to say anything else, it had to be in tongues. Finally, around 6pm that evening, my spirit quietened down. I was still so full of joy, but very tired.

"That was the beginning of my relationship with the Holy Spirit; He became my best friend from then on. Although as I got older, He stopped telling me the meaning of difficult words, He just asked me to get a dictionary instead. I guess God just wanted me to learn how to wait on Him, even from an early age.

"Together, my parents were a formidable force. They taught us to love the Lord with all our hearts, they taught us God's word and what I loved the most was that they let us make our mistakes. Some mistakes required the 'rod of correction' if you know what I mean, but our home was never short of love. Mum always had worship music or the Word playing in the house, and that created a warm, Godly atmosphere. When people worked into our house, they'd always say the same thing, they'd say 'every time we come into your house Debby (that's my mum's name), we feel like there's nothing to fear, there's so much peace here.' 'That's my Jesus,' Mum would say.

"Uncle John came to visit every Christmas, he was fun and he and Dad got on like a house of fire. Our parents taught us right from wrong, they taught us to be led by the Holy Spirit, it wasn't always easy growing up in my house, but we knew without a shadow of a doubt that we were loved.

Chapter 3
School Days

"Sam and I got into the same secondary school and our parents were really glad, they thought we could watch out for each other since it was a boarding school. It was just a few miles from home, but our parents thought we should give boarding school a try; 'it toughens you up' Dad said. Now, in our house, no one makes a move without asking God first, so of course my parents sought the Lord on this and the answer was yes, He (God) chose the school by the way, and we got well above the required grades and so got scholarships to the school. It wasn't a Christian school, but it was one of the best in Virginia.

"It was interesting mixing with the other students and making new friends. Sam and I had no problems sharing our faith with our new friends and anyone who was interested, including our classmates and teachers. Most people enjoyed listening to us talk about Jesus, but a few of them just didn't want to know, and we were okay with that. Mum taught us never to go against people's will because God does not do that, she said 'keep showing them love and they'll come around.'

"Our first term was very exciting, although we missed home so much. We spent most of our allowance calling home and we couldn't wait for the holidays so we could see our parents again. Sam and I set up a club, we called it 'His Fun Club' and, over the weekend, we used one of the classrooms for our Fun Club activities. We wanted to do something fun with other students, we wanted people to know that loving the Lord can be loads of fun. We organised different activities including; singing and dancing competitions, bible-based double jeopardy, movie night and anything else we could think of. The students loved it, and soon our Club membership grew and even teachers got involved as they had to supervise some of our activities. Sam suggested creating membership cards and choosing leaders who could be in charge of different aspects of the Club. Everyone who joined the Club understood that whatever we did had to be bible-based. We prayed, worshiped and had fun in the Lord and everyone loved it.

"We even had a Homework Club, this was an idea I got from the Holy Spirit one day when I got stuck with my geography homework. He said, 'Why don't you find one of your classmates who is really good at geography and see if he or she can help you and, in turn, you find out what subject they aren't so good at and see if that's your strength and you can offer to help them with that.' So I did exactly what He said and soon I had buddied up with Mark Gibson for geography. He helped me with geography while I helped him with maths. People got interested in this new system so I made it one of the Club's activities; we studied for tests together and had mock exams as well.

"We had loads of fun, although, being teenagers, we had a lot of issues to deal with. So many things that we hadn't been exposed to at home suddenly confronted us, like being attracted to the opposite sex; I thought it was just me, but after I spoke to Sam about it (we're really close like that), I discovered it wasn't just me after all. Mum was more prepared for this than we were, so she wrote us letters with a few scriptures to guide us. It was

Holy Spirit Diaries

quite difficult as some of our friends did not have the moral views we had and this sometimes made me feel like they had all the fun and I couldn't, but the Holy Spirit kept encouraging me and teaching me God's principles concerning dating and sex. When I saw all the heartache some of my girlfriends put themselves through because of their boyfriends, I gave thanks to God and I could see why God wanted me to wait until I was wise enough to make certain decisions and mature enough to control my emotions. The Holy Spirit always said to me, 'Dassah, you have to learn to control your emotions and know not to be led by them.' He gave me *proverbs 25:28*; *whoever has no rule over his own spirit is like a city broken down, without walls (NKJV)*. When I studied that scripture further, I discovered that the word 'spirit' also referred to emotions. I learnt that I had to be lead by the Spirit of God and not by what I felt. It wasn't always easy to say no to my emotions, but the Holy Spirit made it easier by helping me practice and rewarding me each time I listened to Him over my emotions. For example, He had always told me not to stay out later than 10pm and not to spend longer than 15 minutes on the phone with a boy after 9pm. One night, a boy that I really liked called me after 9.30pm and as soon as it was 9.42pm I heard Him say, 'It's time to say goodbye to him', but I was very reluctant to do this. I obeyed anyway and I made sure I was off the phone by 9.45pm. He said He was proud of me and one day soon I would understand why He gave me this rule. Well, this guy called me frequently at about the same time and I was always sure to say goodbye after 15 minutes. One day, he walked up to me at lunchtime and said, 'You're not like the other girls, not even some of the other Christian girls, you're different.' When I asked why he said, 'Well, you have principles and you do not bend or break them for any reason. I have spent many nights on the phone with other girls and we talk for hours on end without saying anything meaningful, we don't gain anything from our conversation, but with you, I learn a lot. There's just something about you.' I was so happy, but of course I didn't let it show too much. Yup! God taught me how not to present myself cheaply, not to come across as available and that way I won't attract men of unsavoury character."

"Hold on a minute, what do you mean? The Holy Spirit taught you about His principles concerning sex?" I asked.

"Well I had seen some of my friends kissing on the lips, the way my parents did when they thought we weren't looking and I was curious. So I asked the Holy Spirit if I could kiss my boyfriend like that, when I had one. I'll never forget that conversation; it went something like this.

"Dassah: 'Lord, can I ask you something?'
Holy Spirit: 'You know you can ask me anything.'
Dassah: 'Well when I have a boyfriend, can I kiss him?'
Holy Spirit: 'Of course you can.'
Dassah: 'Really?'
Holy Spirit: 'Well yes, why do you sound so surprised?'
Dassah: 'I just didn't think it would be right.'
Holy Spirit: 'There's nothing wrong with kissing a boy on the cheek is there?'
Dassah: 'No! I meant on the lips; you know what I meant Lord.'
Holy Spirit: 'Aahhh! Well you have the answer to that one already, you see; I let you answer that yourself, a few seconds ago when you said you didn't think it would be right. Child! Most of

the time, you know on the inside what's right, but as with many of my children, you want to work or talk your way out of doing the right thing, just to satisfy your flesh. Your Spirit tells you that kissing like your parents before you are married isn't right, you just don't know why it isn't right yet.'

Dassah: 'So why is it wrong?'

Holy Spirit: 'Do you remember your neighbour's wedding that you attended last year?'

Dassah: 'Yeeessss?'

Holy Spirit: 'Well what did the pastor say to the groom and bride before they kissed?'

Dassah: 'You may kiss the bride?!'

Holy Spirit: 'Well that statement suggests that permission was being given for the groom to kiss his bride. The groom can now kiss his bride however he wants because her body belongs to him and his body belongs to his bride.'

Dassah: 'So prior to that day he didn't have permission to kiss her like that!'

Holy Spirit: 'When they kiss like that, there is also an exchange of bodily fluids, which signifies that they have become one before God and man (a covenant) and then the consummation of the marriage afterwards (lovemaking) which leads to a soul tie. That couple is now legally one in the spirit realm. What many young people are doing today is they get themselves tied down spiritually with different partners and they end up with a lot of spiritual and emotional baggage, sometimes even physical baggage [diseases]. It is a sin before God to have sex before marriage but most young Christians don't intentionally want to sin against God, they just don't understand the implication of such actions and they haven't been taught the fear of the Lord. ***Proverbs 16:6 say; and by the fear of the Lord, one departs from evil***

(KJV). You see Dassah, the problem isn't just the kissing, when a two young unmarried Christians kiss like that, within a few minutes, their thought pattern changes. Whilst they may not have thought of sex beforehand because they know it's a sin, they are thinking of it whilst kissing, their emotions take over and of course the enemy is always ready to pervert the pure and so they take it a bit further than they planned. They keep going further until they find themselves in bed together, you understand?

'See **Song of Solomon 2: 7**; *I charge you, O daughters of Jerusalem, By the gazelles or by the does of the field, Do not stir up nor awaken love until it pleases.* This scripture is mentioned a few times in that book.

'You have to guard your heart and mind with all diligence, be careful what you see, hear and what you allow yourself to feel, all this can affect your thought life and the battle starts in the mind. You have to present yourself as a living sacrifice to God daily, you can't do that easily with thoughts of sex on your mind can you? Sooner or later, the enemy will make you feel guilty for having such thoughts, and then he places you in bondage, all because of a kiss with a boy you may never marry. Now tell me Dassah, is that kiss worth your spiritual and emotional freedom, your relationship with God and your peace? There is time for everything child.'

Dassah: 'Now I understand, I can't say it isn't tempting, but I have a level of understanding about the subject now, and I know to be careful.'

"It was our final year and we had just come back from the Christmas holidays. We had the university entrance exams ahead of us and we also had a lot of applications to fill out. Sam and I were hoping to get scholarships for our respective universities.

Sam had chosen MIT as he wanted to major in engineering, I on the other had chosen Yale, these were our first choices, and we had others. We knew we weren't going to end up in the same universities, seeing as we both wanted to study different subjects. I was interested in studying anything to do with counselling people, but I wanted to do a major degree first, so I decided on psychology. The Holy Spirit suggested it so I went to find out more about it and saw that it could be a stepping stone to the type of career I wanted."

Chapter 4
Why Lord?

"One night, God woke me up to pray for my parents, I didn't know what to pray, and so I just prayed in tongues. I prayed for over two hours until I felt peaceful and then I went back to sleep. The next day, during lunch, Sam came over to tell me of his experience, it turned out that He was woken up by God to pray for Mum and Dad too, and so were two of our friends.

"During one of our classes that afternoon, the principal called for Sam and I, and we just knew something was wrong. I held Sam's hand really tight and we were praying in tongues under our breath, asking the Lord for strength.

"When we got to the principal's office, we saw our neighbour, Mr Johnson, there. We knew that whatever was coming next could not be good. I have never felt so queasy in my life before, I thought I was going to be sick and throw up all over the principal's office. I could hear the Holy Spirit saying 'peace, be still'. Mr Fitch, the principal, opened his mouth and it felt like no words came out, I just couldn't hear a word he said, but I could see his mouth moving and just about make out the words 'are dead'. I understood alright, what he was saying. I fell backwards and Mr Johnson caught me. Mum and Dad had been in an accident and were dead. I could feel my heart beating so fast it felt like it was about to break through my ribcage. I felt like screaming, but it seemed all the strength I had in me had vanished with the word 'dead'. It couldn't be true, I had just prayed! God still answers prayers doesn't He? I felt like a million thoughts were racing through my mind all at once, like what did they do to deserve this? What did Sam and I do to deserve this, wasn't God on our side anymore? I had no strength to stand; my legs were shaking so bad it hurt. The principal tried to console me, I didn't want consolation, I wanted to remain on the floor in the arms of Mr Johnson until he took his words back! I looked over at Sam. He was silent. He looked numb. He didn't utter a word, but seemed to accept this death sentence pronounced on our parents so easily. I heard myself mumbling the words 'Wake me up, I don't like this dream, please wake me up, Mum? Dad? Wake me up.' It was obvious that this was no dream, I could hear Mr Johnson saying, 'It's okay Dassah, it's okay,' as I cried bitterly.

"Mum and Dad died in June 1980, when Sam and I were 17 years old. That year was so hard for us both, if there was a time I thought of turning away from God, it was then. I felt like all hope was lost, I couldn't believe God would let them die just like that, at least I thought He was the one that let them die. Sam tried his best to be strong, but I could see he was hurting. Neither of us wanted to pray, we just didn't know what to say to God, we were just so angry and disappointed with Him. I could still hear the Holy Spirit saying, 'I'm here when you need me, whenever you're ready to talk, I'm right here. I'm not letting you go.'

"Uncle John came to the US three days after my parents' death and he wanted to take us back to the UK. The principal said that we could defer our exams for a year if we wanted to, but Sam and I decided to sit the exams that year. We didn't want to have to come back a year later to deal with the memories. So

Uncle John took a few months off work and stayed in our house till we sat our exams. Our friends were very supportive and you remember the guy that said I wasn't like other girls? His name was David Elliot, yeah! He looked after me, he helped with my school work and he was just there, although I never spoke to him about what happened; he knew not to ask any questions, he was just there for me.

"I didn't speak to the Holy Spirit much after that, I just couldn't.

Chapter 5
Healing

"Our exams were in August, just two months after the tragedy. A few days before my exams, I woke up suddenly, I felt a tickle on the sole of my right foot; it was as if someone was drawing on the sole of my foot with a finger. I checked underneath my duvet to see if there was a simple explanation, but there wasn't, there was just this overwhelming presence, it was so powerful and it wasn't scary at all, it was just powerful with a sense of deep love. I knew the Lord was in my room. I got out of my bed and knelt down and as soon as I got on my knees, I began to weep. I wept so much I thought I was going to run out of air, I couldn't breathe. When I finished crying I sang a worship song Mum had taught me, 'Let your living water flow over my soul.' The presence of God was even stronger and I could barely move. After I finished singing, His presence lifted and I went back to sleep.

"This happened to me three nights in a row and, on the third night, I was able to speak to God and I asked; 'Why did you take them?'

He said, 'I didn't.'

I was shocked, 'What do you mean you didn't, you're God and nothing happens without your say so.'

'I need you to read *1 Samuel, chapter 30* and we'll talk some more about this,' He said.

Yewande Erinle

"The next day was Sunday, so I woke up that morning and picked up my bible. I hadn't read it since my parents had died, and I hadn't been to church since then either. I studied the scripture God had given me, and I sensed the presence of the Holy Spirit so strongly in my room, it was like electricity all over my body. I understood that scripture in a way I never understood it before. I could see for the first time that we have an enemy who is strongly against everything we stand for. He is against our joy and happiness and he will do anything to steal that away from us, he is so jealous of our relationship with God that he works hard to destroy it; he works hard to destroy our faith in God. In the scripture the Holy Spirit had given me, David had gone to war, he was going about doing God's business, he was a Godly man just like Mum and Dad were, but the enemy hated him and wanted to steal from him. The enemy wanted to destroy all that David had, including his faith in God and maybe eventually kill him. God was there when the enemy went into David's camp to raid it. David could have blamed God for the disaster that had struck the camp, after all, his men blamed him, so shouldn't he blame God? But he didn't, he knew exactly who to blame for this and with God's permission he went after the enemy. The Holy Spirit also took me to the book of Job and, after studying the whole book, I saw how the enemy tried to destroy Job's life by taking everything Job had including his health, wealth and family, but Job refused to give up, he refused to curse God and die. Yes! He was distressed and he got so confused that he didn't even know who God was anymore or what God stands for, but he still refused to curse God. Satan wants to attack our relationship with God by causing us to lose our faith and turn away from Him, and he does this by attacking us and those we love. In all of this, God tells us to be watchful and pray always,

He tells us to be vigilant of this enemy that is moving to and fro looking for souls to destroy, the Lord expects us to be on our guard at all times. We must understand that our faith in God is very important, and that's what the enemy wants; once he gets that, he has us where he wants. If you remember what Jesus said in **Luke 18:8b** *Nevertheless when the Son of man cometh, shall He find faith on the earth?* This shows us how important our faith is to God. Jesus also shows us in another scripture (**Luke 22:31-32**) that the attacks of the enemy are against our faith and nothing else. The devil does not want or need our money, property, health and so on, but if he can cause us to lose faith in Abba Father, he's won the battle, because he knows that without faith 'no man can please God', see **Hebrews 11:6** *But without faith it is impossible to please Him: for he that cometh to God must believe that He is, and that He is a rewarder of them that diligently seek Him.* Our relationship with God is faith-based.

Luke 22: ³¹*And the Lord said, Simon, Simon, behold,* **Satan hath desired to have you, that he may sift you as wheat:** ³²***But I have prayed for thee, that thy faith fail not:*** *and when thou art converted, strengthen thy brethren (KJV).* Here, Jesus tells Simon the devil has desired to sift him, to shake him, to cause him grief, but then Jesus says, 'He has prayed for Simon's faith not to fail, as long as Simon's faith is strong and firm, he will not be sifted or moved or shaken. As long as our faith is strong, we will not be moved, no matter what the devil throws at us.' I believe that Jesus is interceding for us in heaven for our faith not to fail; I truly believe that this is probably the only prayer He is praying.

"I immediately phoned Sam and asked him to come to my room. As soon as he came in, I gave him the scripture and I asked him to read it, I told him what I had learnt and also used Job's example. When we finished, he began to weep, the power of God hit him right there and he fell on his face weeping before the Lord. We both understood that it wasn't God's perfect will for our parents to die in that car accident, God did not ask that drunk driver to get behind his wheel that morning knowing he was drunk. That drunk driver drove right into Mum and Dad's car, killing them all instantly, leaving both his family and ours mourning our loss. This was definitely not God's perfect will, but He is able to turn it around. Although we still felt that God could have worked some sort of miracle to save our parents, we knew the devil was to blame for this and we refused to let him steal our relationship with God.

"Sam and I talked properly for the first time about what happened. It was amazing that we both felt the same way, we were hurting so badly, but we had bottled it all up and refused to talk about it with anyone, including the Holy Spirit, our best friend. When we finished talking, we worshipped a little and we felt a lot better. We still didn't have a full understanding of what happened and why God had not intervened to save our parents, but we knew that God did not do this and that someday we'd have a better understanding of the events surrounding that accident. Before Sam left my room, we prayed and asked the Lord to forgive us for being angry with Him, and that He should restore unto us what we had lost, our parents. We also prayed for the drunk driver and his family, we asked God to help us forgive him and we asked Him to look after his family.

"We had our exams that week; I had five papers to sit whilst Sam had six. We studied hard together and with the members of our Club. They were surprised to see us back to the Homework Club, but they said they had been praying for us and they knew God would not let us go. It was Friday and our exams were over, we had a party to celebrate this. I went to the party with David and Sam, we had fun. It was our first proper outing since our parents had died. We stayed there for about two hours and found it too overwhelming, so we went back to Sam's room. The supervisors had moved curfew from 10pm to 1am for the seniors, because it was our last week of school and we were graduating.

"That night, in Sam's room, David asked us how we could still love God after everything and we simply said, 'We don't know, He just helps us love Him, we have no love of our own, it comes from God.' We told David that we understood that it wasn't God that killed our parents; we explained things to him as best we could and took him to the scriptures. Finally, he stood up and said, 'I want what you've got, that thing that makes you joyful even in the most depressing circumstances, yes, that thing, I want it now.' Sam took David to *John, chapter 3*, and we taught him from the Word of God; it was so amazing, tears streamed down his face when we told him about Jesus dying for us. We knew the Holy Spirit was at work because we had shared the same scriptures with other students before and did not get this type of reaction. Anyway, David gave his life to Christ that night and asked to be baptised and so Sam baptised him in his bathroom that night—well, God was there too.

"The weekend came and it was time to say our goodbyes until graduation day, which was in April the next year. Sam and I had to go back to England with Uncle John and we were a bit reluctant because we were going to miss everyone and we weren't sure what England would be like for us. I was going to miss David very much, but I knew that our paths would cross again. Uncle John was waiting for us at the school reception, we were so glad to see him. I hugged him so tightly, he begged me to let go, 'You're cutting off my air supply,' he cried, jokingly. We hadn't spoken to him properly since the incident and we knew he wanted to talk about it but wasn't sure if we were ready. Sam suggested that we all go somewhere quiet for dinner and Uncle John agreed. We talked and cried, we told Uncle John of our experience with God and He told us how God had been faithful to him through it all. He said he had got engaged in June and wanted to surprise Mum and Dad with the news before they died. Like us, he too was a little angry with God, because not only had his sister and brother-in law died, he felt God allowed his parents to die in that fire so many years ago too. He said his fiancée, Bola (she's Nigerian you see, just like you), kept on praying for him and with him, and tried to share the Word with him, but he felt so numb. He said she was very understanding and she never argued with him or forced him to pray or go to church; she mourned with him and gave him space to mourn alone too. He mentioned how God showed him dreams of Bola praying for him.

"By the time we had finished, it was midnight and the restaurant was about to close, we were the only customers left. We hadn't noticed anyone leaving; it was like we were in a world of our own. We had decided to go back to England with Uncle John the next weekend and he agreed that we could come back to the US for our graduation, and we could either choose to go to university in the States or in England. We rented out our house in Virginia, so we could save money for university. We were so grateful that our parents did not believe in mortgages and loans. They had paid for our house in full so we owned it and had some inheritance money that our parents left to us, quite a bit of money actually, but we refused to touch it; we weren't ready for that just yet."

Chapter 6
Uncle John

"Uncle John had a lovely house in Manchester, England, and it was really big. He had four bedrooms, a study, two living rooms and two garages. He said he bought it just before he proposed to Bola, but she was unaware of it. He has a flat a few blocks away and that's where she goes to visit. He wants to give her the deed to the house with her name on it as her wedding present. 'How sweet,' I said.

"Uncle John found us part-time jobs; Sam got one in a construction company where he was able to shadow a real mechanical engineer, and I got a job in the hospital where Uncle John worked, in the Psychiatry ward where my main responsibility was to type up patients' notes. We knew God had a hand in this; we got jobs that prepared us for what we wanted to study at university. This wasn't a coincidence' it was a 'God-incidence'.

"Uncle John and Bola were getting married in November and there was a lot of planning to do, especially with Bola being Nigerian, you do know what I mean don't you? With you being Nigerian I mean; boy, do they love their parties!

"We finally met Bola in September; she wanted to give us enough time to bond with our uncle before meeting us. She was so sweet and the glory of God was all over her, she reminded me so much of Mum, except of course she had this lovely black African skin that never seemed to age. She was gorgeous and Sam and I could see why Uncle John loved her. In fact, I can tell you now that Sam had a little crush on her; for the first few weeks, he wouldn't look straight at her whilst talking to her, he always looked downwards. It was funny to watch, but he soon got over it when he met Linda. Linda was Sam's boss's daughter and he says it was love at first sight, but I say there's no such thing.

"Linda was a born-again Christian and she took us to her church, a Pentecostal church in Bradford, which was not too far from Manchester. She was a no-nonsense girl, very well-disciplined, but loved to have fun. We got on well, although we didn't always agree on everything, we loved each other. She was my best friend and still is.

"November came round really fast and soon it was Uncle John's wedding day. I had never seen so many people at one wedding; he had over 400 guests and 350 of them were Bola's family, friends and colleagues. It was so beautiful. Bola had to change her Nigerian outfit a few times; it was the custom that the couple showed themselves off in different expensive attire. Uncle John had to wear the Nigerian traditional clothes too. He looked so cute in them and it was obvious that he enjoyed wearing them. Bola's parent were pastors in Nigeria, which explained about 150 of the guests at the reception, the others were just family and friends. Bola was an only child.

"Sam and I had to give a toast at the reception, and we hadn't really understood what Uncle John and Bola meant to us till then, they were like parents to us. It was then that I realised that God answered our prayer, the one Sam and I prayed after our parents died, that God should restore to us what we had lost? Yes, God had answered our prayers. You know that scripture that says, *all things work together for good for them that love God?*

***Romans 8:28** And we know that all things work together for good to them that love God, to them who are the called according to his purpose.*

"Well God made sure that we didn't lack parental love. We still missed our parents a lot, but we loved having Bola and Uncle John as parents. Bola was a great mum to us and her parents were like the grandparents we never had.

"Uncle John and Bola went off to Tahiti for their honeymoon, they were gone for a week and we spent that week with Bola's parents. They weren't going back to Nigeria till the newlyweds got back from their honeymoon.

"We learnt so much that week from our new grandparents, it was enlightening. They taught us about generational curses and covenants and how to break them, we also learnt about warfare prayers. It was something we hadn't been exposed to and I truly believe that God brought the Lawals (that was their surname) over to teach us more about our authority and responsibilities as Christians. We learnt more about the power we had as Christians and how to use it when we pray. During this week, we understood a bit more about the death of our parents and even our grandparents, and we knew we had to ensure that it won't repeat itself in our generation or in the generations to come. We allowed the Holy Spirit to teach us a bit more about this and give us a few examples in the Bible, and He gave us a few prayer points as well. Our new grandparents prayed for us too. It was a whole week of fasting and praying, and we enjoyed every moment.

"Uncle John and Bola got back from their honeymoon and we were so happy to see them. I missed Bola so much and I couldn't wait to hear about her week away. She booked a table for two at a really nice Italian restaurant and said we had a lot of catching up to do. I couldn't say no to a free Italian meal, so we went out while Sam stayed home with Uncle John and Bola's parents. Bola's parents went back to Nigeria the week after and the newlyweds returned to work.

Chapter 7
That Time of Year

"After the wedding, I started to miss David more and more. We talked a few times a week, but it was difficult not being able to see him. With the wedding over, I was less busy so I guess I had a lot more time to think about him.

"The last week of November was Thanksgiving in America; it was a surprise to us that it wasn't celebrated here in England. We missed our parents even more at this time so, after much thought, Sam and I decided to throw a Thanksgiving party to celebrate our parents' passing on into glory. Sam and I cooked and we invited all our friends and neighbours.

"It was a tradition in our family that, at the dinner table on Thanksgiving Day, everyone would say what they are most thankful for. So we asked everyone to say one thing they were most thankful to God for. When it was my turn, I said I was most thankful for the new family that God had given Sam and I. Uncle John was most thankful for God's love that was shown in many ways through different people and Sam, well, I really can't remember specifically what he was most thankful for, because he gave a really long speech that evening, but I know that I summarised it in my head as 'thankful for family'.

"David called that evening to wish me happy Thanksgiving. He said he was now teaching Sunday school and working part-time in a fancy restaurant; he loved to cook you see, and his goal was to become a chef and own his own restaurant someday. He said he was trying to save up enough money to come and visit. The Holy Spirit had extended the length of my calls by ten minutes, since we were so far apart and only got to speak two or three times a week. Actually, I negotiated with Him and I was allowed ten minutes if we spent five minutes praying together. I prayed for Him every day, as many times a day as I remembered.

"Soon it was Christmas; this was a little bit easier than Thanksgiving. We spent Christmas delivering food, presents and bibles to the homeless and the sick people in hospitals, it was Bola's ministry, she did this every year and this time she asked if we wanted to join in and we were delighted to help. We had never done anything like that before; it was a new experience for us. It was so emotional to see the look on the faces of some of the people we blessed, sometimes they hugged us and wept and other times they were so moved by the love that they just stared at us in shock. I cried so much, I'd never seen so many people in pain or lack before, I found myself being very grateful to God and also praying for healing and provision for those that needed it. I knew that day, that I wanted to minister to people's needs, but what I didn't know was how."

Chapter 8
Surprise!

"January 1981 came really fast and Sam and I were expecting our exam results and letters of acceptance to the universities of our choice. We had a lot to look forward to, including our eighteenth birthday in February, although we planned to celebrate it quietly.

"Our results came by post on 13th January and Sam and I did very well. Sam got the grades for his first choice and got on the scholarship scheme for MIT and, although I got the grades for my first choice, I did not get on their scholarship scheme, but I wasn't disappointed, I knew God would provide. We decided we would go back to America for our university education, we knew that this was what the Lord wanted, and Bola and Uncle John agreed. We signed off on our acceptance letters and registered online for our courses. Uncle John and Bola took us out for a celebratory dinner at the end of the month and they bought us driving lessons as well as a car between us, for when we passed our test. I was so happy that I cried and I hoped Mum and Dad could see how happy we were.

It was 18th February, our birthday. Linda had come over with her presents for Sam and me. We also had presents from Uncle John and Bola. Bola told me there was a surprise for me later that evening, but I didn't think much of it. I was excited and kept on guessing, but there weren't any clues. I even asked the Holy Spirit, but He simply said, 'If I told you it wouldn't be a surprise now, would it?' Although I knew He wasn't going to tell me, I just thought there was no harm in trying.

"I got a phone call from David; he wished me happy birthday and prayed for me over the phone. He said he baked a lovely cake for me, red velvet, and he was going to share it with his friends and family in honour of my birthday. He spoke to Sam as well. *I can't wait till graduation to see David again* I thought and I heard the Holy Spirit laugh.
'What's funny?' I asked.
'Nothing,' He said, 'can't I laugh when I want to?'
'Yes, you can, Lord, and what did you get me for my birthday this year? You know it's a big one, Lord, what are you giving me?' I asked.
'You'll see,' He said, 'just be patient.'

"That evening, Linda said she'd treat us to a Chinese takeaway, so she left at about 5.30pm to pick up our order. At 6pm, the doorbell rang, 'That's Linda with our food,' I said. 'I'll get it'. When I opened the door, there was a young man standing there with his back to me.

'Can I help you?' I asked, and he said, 'Yes' and turned round. I nearly passed out; it was David standing there with a cake box in his hand. I immediately heard the Holy Spirit say 'Happy birthday darling.' I screamed 'Thank you Lord!' and hugged David. It was such a surprise that I couldn't find any words for the next fifteen minutes. I felt so special that evening, for once, my birthday wasn't just a day I shared with my twin, I had someone who was there for me, not Sam and I, just me. I was so excited, I could burst, it was as if I had been given a high dose of sugar and I could do a thousand things at once. I was the happiest girl in that house that evening. I felt special in God's eyes; He gave me my heart's desire even though I didn't ask Him for it.

"It was strange though, no one else was surprised, not even Linda, everyone was in on it, even my twin, the closest person to me. I still don't know how He was able to keep the news from me!"

Suddenly, Dassah and I heard a voice behind us saying, "Well, because Uncle John promised me tickets to the next Manchester United football game if I kept quiet, you see."
"Sam! Good to see you, where's Linda?" exclaimed Dassah.
"Sam? Is this Sam, your twin?" I asked.
"Yes" Dassah replied with excitement as she introduced us.
"So how's Linda?" I enquired.
"Yes how's your wife?" added Dassah.
"Wife? You mean he married Linda?" I asked.
"Yes, of course, they have two kids, twins actually."
"Three kids now," Sam replied with a broad smile.
"Oh!" Dassah exclaimed. "She's had the baby!"
"Yes, a few hours ago, just wanted to let you and your hubby know, where is he by the way?"
"Gone to the grocers," Dassah replied, "I'll let him know when he gets back."
"I'll let you get back to the story Dassah. Nice to meet you Dami," Sam said, as he left.

I glanced at my watch and it was 10.15am; I was glad I still had time to hear the rest of the story.

"Where did I stop?" Dassah asked and before I could respond she said, "Oh yes, the surprise gift."

"Sam and I enjoyed our birthday; David brought the red velvet cake he told me about over the phone. It turned out that he wasn't in the States when he called me earlier on that day, He was on the plane. He said to me, 'I told you I was going to share the cake with friends and family' and I laughed. His parents had given him half of the money for his ticket, and Uncle John paid for his hotel accommodation for two weeks.

"I spent the next two weeks with David; we were inseparable every day until bed time when he would leave for his hotel. He was at our door for 10am every morning and since it was his first visit to England, Sam, Linda and I took him everywhere we could think of. We visited London and other well-known tourist cities. We had loads of fun and we made an album as a memoir for David to take back with him.
"The album is here somewhere, oh there it is."
Dassah took me through the album and showed me David.
"Wow!" I said, "he's quite a catch, I see why you liked him so much."

She laughed and said, "We had so much fun together, and we both loved the Lord so much. We had our differences, but we accepted each other. He didn't try to change me, and I never tried to change him either.

"Two weeks were up just like that and it was time for David to go back home. I was a little bit sad, but very grateful to

God for the opportunity to see him again. I knew I would see him in April so I wasn't too upset."

Chapter 9
Graduation

"Our part-time jobs ended in March and we began to make preparations to fly back to America for graduation day. We were so excited; we had missed all our friends so much. Our tickets were booked and we had to sort out accommodation for the period we were there, as our house was still being rented out. Uncle John took care of all that for us.

"Bola and Uncle John flew with us, they attended the graduation ceremony. Seeing everyone again was overwhelming, but in a good way. I was asked to sing at the ceremony; everyone knew I loved to sing and that it was my gift. I sang 'Jesus loves me this I know'. It moved so many people to tears, including Bola; she said she didn't know I could sing like that. Sam was the class valedictorian and he gave a beautiful speech as that was his gift, talking!

"Uncle John and Bola said we could either choose to stay in the States till September when university starts, or come back to England with them. Sam and I talked it over, and since we had open tickets, we decided to spend the rest of April and the whole of May in America, and then go back to England for a few months before coming back for university. Uncle John said we could use some of our inheritance money if we needed too. Sam and I decided that we wanted to travel round the States and Canada, and so we did. It was just Sam and I together again for the first time in a long time. We had fun together and went back to Virginia for our last two weeks. It turned out that Sam missed Linda too much and decided to go home earlier than planned. I stayed in Virginia till the end of May. As you may already have guessed, I spent most of my time with David. I got to know his parents and two older sisters really well. His sisters were twins too.

"My two weeks were up, and I was back in Manchester before I knew it. I was greeted with some great news; Bola was over two months pregnant. I was elated, I was going to have a cousin really soon, I couldn't wait. It was going to be a December baby, Sam and I thought of names for the baby because Bola said it was customary in Nigeria, for the baby's aunty and uncle to choose the name."

Chapter 10
Anniversary

"It was 19th June, exactly one year after Mum and Dad's death. Sam and I wanted to spend it in church; we had Thanksgiving service on that day. We wanted to remember their life on earth and how they lived for Jesus.

"When we got home, I got out our old albums, and we all looked through them. We told Bola all about our parents, since she hadn't met them. There were so many funny incidents that we could remember; like when Mum was having one of those days Sam and I referred to as 'experiment day'. Basically, once or twice a year, she'd pretend we had gone to eat out at a fancy restaurant in another country, for example Italy; she would cook an Italian meal as best as she could and make our living room look very Italian. She went to the extent of writing out comments that she expected Dad and us to say in Italian. We all had to play along, it was ridiculous but we had so much fun. We would come home from school sometimes and find a restaurant in our living room; themes ranged from African to Asian, whatever Mum fancied really.

"I also remembered how much my parents loved each other, and how they treated each other. I learnt from Dad how a man should treat his wife, so I knew what to expect from my future husband. Dad never ever shouted at Mum, no matter how angry he was, and Mum made him very mad sometimes, but he would just go into his study to calm down. He did other things to show he was upset, like skipping a meal or just reading a book in his study, it was our way of knowing what mood he was in. If he was in the study frowning at a book, then we knew it wasn't a good time to ask for anything. Mum never disrespected Dad, at least not around us and not in public. Even when she was right, she would submit to him and his wishes. If he later admitted she was right, I never heard her say, 'I told you so', she would smile at him lovingly and say, 'You just needed time to make up your own mind, there's nothing wrong with that love.' She never made him feel bad for making a mistake, although she could get really upset over certain things, and she knew how to shout.

"If Mum shouted, you knew you were in trouble, and her voice was so loud it made you shake. Dad never had to shout, one stern look from him did it for me. I knew I had to straighten up whenever he gave me the look. It took a bit more than looks for Sam, he was quite set in his ways at times. He always had a good talking to from Dad and received a few punishments. Once, Dad grounded Sam for a whole week and he wasn't allowed to play soccer for a whole month. I tell you, that really hit him hard and he made sure he never did anything to bring on such a harsh punishment again. Sam loves soccer you see, it's his hobby.

"My parents were not perfect, but they were no hypocrites either. They loved the Lord with all their hearts, minds and strength, and it showed. They loved us so much too, we never ran out of hugs and kisses, it was a bit embarrassing at times, but we loved it secretly. Some of our friends were a bit envious of what we had at home, they didn't have that kind of love and they wished they could. Sam and I would invite them round regularly, and our parents showed them love all the time. It was like our family was growing, other kids were always at ours, especially during the festive seasons like Thanksgiving, Christmas and Easter; you name it, our house was full. Mum loved to cook and everyone loved her cooking, she taught Sam and I and a few other friends of ours how to cook too.

"On the anniversary of their death, we celebrated their life and what they stood for and we tried to recount all the lovely memories, especially the funny ones. Oh! I haven't told you about the breast milk incident. Dad drank breast milk thinking it was fresh milk! You see, one of Mum's friends came to stay over after having her baby, her husband had travelled and Mum said she'd look after her till he got back. The lady, Aunty Diane, had expressed some milk in a bottle, but the bottle didn't look like a feeding bottle, it had a regular top on it. Anyway, Dad came home from night duty early one morning and he wanted a glass of milk, so he grabbed the bottle and poured the milk into his cup. He drank it and went off to bed. Aunty Diane came downstairs to get the milk for the baby later on that day, only to discover it was gone. Mum knew immediately what had happened and couldn't stop laughing. We all waited till Dad got up and Mum asked him if he had some milk that morning and whether it tasted a little different. Dad said that he did and that he thought the milk tasted different but he put it down to Mum having changed the type of milk she bought. We all burst out laughing until *someone* had the courage to tell him that it was breast milk—that someone was me. My God, you should have seen the expression on his face; he ran up to the bathroom to throw up, but the milk was long gone.

Yewande Erinle

"We missed mum and dad on the anniversary of their passing on to glory, but we were thankful to have known them as our physical and spiritual parents. They taught us a lot."

Chapter 11
A Miracle—The Power of Prayer

"Early one afternoon, that summer, we heard a scream followed by a thump; it sounded like someone had fallen. Bola was in her room and Sam and I were watching telly downstairs. We ran upstairs to Bola's room and found her stretched out on the floor. She had passed out and was bleeding. We immediately began to pray and the Lord said, 'Call an ambulance immediately, do not panic, just prophesise that the baby will not die but live.' So we did as we were told, and began to prophesise over her till the paramedics arrived.

"When the paramedics arrived, Bola was carried into the ambulance and taken to the hospital. Uncle John was at work in the same hospital, so we had to call him to let him know what had happened, we didn't want him finding out by seeing his wife being brought into the E.R. on a stretcher. Sam phoned to let him know and we drove down to the hospital.

"It was mid-August and Bola was about five months pregnant. I wasn't sure what was happening and Sam and I prayed all the way to the hospital. Bola was already in an examination room by the time we got there, we weren't allowed to see her. Uncle John was with her, so we just waited in the lounge. It was one

Yewande Erinle

of the longest waits of my life, I found myself bargaining with God, asking Him to save her and the baby. Then I remembered the prayer Bola's parents taught us, 'Affliction shall not arise the second time', and Sam and I began to pray against every plan of the enemy, we pled the blood of Jesus against every plan of the enemy, against every spirit that wanted to steal Bola's joy. We declared the Word of God over that baby and its mother. We prayed in tongues for a while and both of us suddenly started to pray against miscarriage, we kept on saying, 'Bola you will not cast your young, the Lord will remove sickness from the midst of thee in Jesus' name'. I didn't know that those were scriptures, Sam and I just kept on saying those words and then I heard the words 'placenta previa' and I immediately prayed against it. We then praised God for bringing His Word concerning Bola and her baby to pass, and thanked Him for answering our prayers and putting the enemy to shame.

"Almost two hours after we got to the hospital, Uncle John came out. He looked exhausted. 'Bola and the baby are fine,' he said. Those words were like music to my ears. I jumped for joy and we had a group hug. We were all so thankful to God. Uncle John said it was a divine intervention, the doctor examining her had already suggested removing the baby because they could no longer hear its heartbeat and Bola was in danger as well. He went to prepare for theatre, but by the time he got back, things had miraculously improved, the baby's heart rate could now be seen and heard on the monitor, and Bola was responding well too. We knew it was our prayers, we were declaring the Word of God at the time the doctor was preparing for surgery, and God turned things around in no time at all. Uncle John said Bola had a high grade of placenta previa and it was quite dangerous for her and the baby, but after their vital signs improved, the doctor did a final examination of the placenta and it had repositioned itself correctly. It was amazing; Sam and I told Uncle John what had happened when we were praying, how the Holy Spirit directed us in prayers.

"I was so grateful to God for not allowing sorrow into our home. I was grateful that Bola's parents had taught us how to pray with faith, power and authority. Sam and I knew that we were now on another level in our walk with God, and that we had to study the word and pray more too.

"Bola had to stay in hospital for a week and, every day, Sam, Linda, Uncle John and I declared the Word of God. When David called, we would pray over the phone for Bola and the baby too."

Chapter 12
Goliath

"Sam and I left for university in the second week of September. Sam left for Cambridge, Massachusetts, and I left for Washington, D.C. It was the first time we would be apart for a while but we were okay with that; we promised to stay in touch and see each other during the holidays.

"David had decided to take a two-year cookery course which required that he spend the first year at a college in Italy and the second one in a top restaurant in France. I wasn't too happy about it, but I knew that God's Will would be done. He promised to come and visit whenever he could. David's course wasn't starting till October, so we saw each other every weekend till he left.

"After David left, I found myself thinking more about where our relationship was going. I wondered if he was the man God wanted for me. I tried not to dwell too much on those thoughts, my excuse was I was only eighteen and there was more than enough time to think of marriage later. I need to just take one day at a time I said to myself.

"I worked hard at university and got an internship with one of my professors who owned a clinic. I was so happy working at her clinic and, to top it all, my Professor, Dr. Susan Reece, was a Christian too. She was a youth pastor in her church and she invited me over for Sunday worship. I enjoyed worshipping at the church that Sunday and I asked God if it could be my home church while I was studying in Washington. I really loved working with Susan. I got to know her husband and kids really well, and she was like a big sister to me. I learnt a lot from her, not just within the university walls, but outside too. Both she and her husband looked out for me a lot; they invited me over for weekends and made sure that I was comfortable. They knew about my relationship with David too and they counselled me.

"December came pretty fast and I got a call from Uncle John, it was good news. The baby had arrived and it was a girl. Bola's mum had come over from Nigeria to help. They named the baby Esther after me (well, the English version) and Bola asked if I could be her godmother. I was so happy; I couldn't wait till my next visit to England. I phoned Sam to see whether he had heard the news and, of course, he had. I called David to give him the good news too. He called me 'the godmother' from then on.

"Sam and I had decided to go back to our house in Virginia for Christmas. The tenants had left and we had advised the estate agents not to take in any new tenants till the following January. It was hard being back at home even though it didn't look much like home anymore; it had been renovated and had new furniture. This was done before the tenants came in. Linda came over from England for Christmas; it was nice having her over for two weeks. Her dad had an apartment a few miles away from us and she stayed there. We had a girls' weekend out the week she arrived; we went shopping and saw a movie. Sam loved Linda very much, it was obvious to me, but he was careful not to show it for some reason, I guess he didn't know much about relationships, since Linda was his first and only girlfriend. Neither of us had any firsthand experience on relationships, what we knew was what we learnt from our parents, Uncle John and Aunty Bola, and of course the Holy Spirit. What we learnt from the Holy Spirit was more than enough though.

"Susan and her family invited us over for Christmas dinner; it was lovely having a big family dinner, although it made us miss Uncle John and Bola more. Christmas day was fun; we suggested visiting an orphanage to Susan and her husband, and they were very interested. Susan knew an orphanage ten miles away from her house, so she called to ask if we could come over with gifts for the children and she was told it was okay. Susan's kids offered to give some of their presents (that in itself was very sweet, I couldn't believe they did that) and we went out to buy some more. Susan's husband also donated some money to the orphanage. Something really bothered me that night at the orphanage; there was a baby girl there, about six weeks old whose mum had abandoned her on the doorstep of the orphanage. She was so beautiful, and I wondered how any mother could abandon their baby, let alone a baby as gorgeous as Lisa (the matron named her Lisa after the Mona Lisa. She said she had a beautiful smile and she was right). I have prayed for Lisa every day since then.

"The holidays were over and we were back at university, Linda had gone back to England too. I had some exams ahead of me, so I had to work even harder than usual. I joined a study group; it kind of reminded me of our Homework Club back at school in Virginia, except this was even more serious. Bola sent me Esther's photos and I put them up in my room, and every day I laid my hands on one of the photos and prophesied over her.

"I hadn't heard from David in three weeks, and he wasn't picking up any of my calls. I started to worry and began to pray for him. I hadn't prayed for him seriously before, but I felt the urgency and a heavy burden in my spirit to intercede diligently for him, so I started to fast and pray. I wasn't sure what I was praying for, the Holy Spirit just said to pray in tongues till there was further revelation.

"The focus of my prayer soon changed after three weeks, I was no longer praying for David, I found myself interceding for my husband. It was very strange, I wasn't thinking of getting married and I had no idea who my husband would be, but God wanted me to pray for him and my marriage. I phoned Sam to see if he was praying for his wife, and he said he started praying for his wife a few months ago, but didn't think much of it. I decided to seek the Lord's face on this, and I asked the Holy Spirit why he wanted me to pray for my husband when I didn't have one yet. He said that it was far easier to start praying about such things earlier to gain spiritual insight. He said I shouldn't wait till I get married before I started praying, he reminded me of what happened during Bola's pregnancy, if we had prayed diligently prior to her pregnancy, that situation could have been avoided all together. The Holy Spirit directed me to a book 'The Power of a Praying Wife', and He said that there was a lot I needed to learn about marriage and that my lessons had just started.

"David finally called me, he apologised for not calling for three months, he said he was so busy and just wasn't able to return my calls. I sensed something was wrong as soon as I heard his voice, but I kept quiet and waited for him to speak. He said he'd been going through a lot and was struggling in his walk with God, he had a friend called Maria, she was a Christian too, and she had been encouraging him in the Lord. I wasn't sure where our conversation was leading to, but I could feel my heart beating really fast. David said he thought he had fallen in love with Maria and that he thinks God was leading him to marry her. I was numb; I wasn't sure what to say. I felt like my heart had been ripped out of my chest and trampled on the ground and placed back again. He said he was sorry and asked for my forgiveness and our phone call ended. I wept so hard and I wished Mum was there to take me in her arms and tell me everything would be fine.

"The next morning, I called Sam and told him what had happened, he didn't sound too surprised, but he was disappointed. He asked if I wanted him to come down to Washington, but I said I'd be fine. I felt very hurt and betrayed. I found myself replaying David's words over and over again in my mind. Then I wondered why the Holy Spirit didn't tell me beforehand that this would happen and so I asked Him. He said, 'You have to experience some things for yourself Dassah, if I keep telling you there is trouble ahead and showing you how to avoid it, you'll never learn anything and you'll never experience life. I don't like to see you cry, but life is about crying, laughing, loving and so on, if you try to avoid all this, then you avoid life itself. I'm not asking you to go and get hurt, but sometimes people will hurt you and they don't always mean to hurt you, but they do and you have to forgive. That's what love does. I told you a few weeks ago that your marriage lessons had started; well this is part of it. I didn't want David to hurt you, but he did; I have forgiven him and so must you. The truth is, David still needs your prayers, he may be with someone else now, but I have chosen you to be his intercessor. Dassah, the pain will not last forever and healing comes with forgiveness.' That night I told God that I had forgiven David and that I wanted Him to heal me so I could move on. I felt peace in my heart that night, even though I was still hurting.

"I went to Susan's house that weekend. I thought I'd surprise her but she wasn't in. Her husband, Alan, was in though, he invited me in but I was reluctant to stay without Susan being there, but I did. He asked why I looked so unhappy and I just broke down crying, I told him everything that had happened between David and me, and what God had told me. He prayed with me and said everything will work out for good. As soon as Susan came back, Alan gave her the news and she gave me the motherly hug I so desired. I wept some more. They asked me to stay over that night and Susan said I could stay home from lectures the next day if I didn't feel up to it.

"The Holy Spirit woke me up at 8 am the next morning and said I should either go for my lectures or go home, but I felt too tired and just didn't obey. I'd never done that before, disobey God I mean, I don't know why I did that. He woke me up two more times, but I just didn't listen to Him. When I got up finally, Susan had gone to work, the kids had gone to school and it was just Alan at home. He asked how I was feeling and I replied jokingly 'I'll live' (well, the English version). He said it was good to see me smile again and we talked for a really long time and I felt better. I started thinking about how nice Alan was and how lucky Susan was to have such a loving man. He gave me a hug as I was leaving and said he'd call to check on me.

"Alan called that evening to check on me and I spoke with Susan as well, they said they were praying for me. Alan started to call me regularly, at first I was a bit uncomfortable and I always let Susan know that Alan had called, but after a while, it felt okay. His calls became more frequent and lasted much longer, and I noticed that I started to like him much more. I prayed about it and God said to stop the phone calls, but I enjoyed speaking to him and he helped me forget about David. He made comments about how beautiful I was and also said that David didn't know what he had lost. I noticed that we didn't talk about God that much anymore, and my prayer life started dwindling. One day, Alan came to see me; he said he had to speak with me. Everything within me knew that this wasn't right, but I was curious to hear what he had to say, so I let him in. I asked him if Susan knew where he was, and he said yes, but I felt he was lying. He told me that he just wanted to see how I was doing and that he brought my favourite ice cream.

"We spoke for over an hour, I can't even remember what we spoke about. He suddenly leaned over to kiss me, when the phone rang and we both jumped. It was Uncle John on the phone, he said the Holy Spirit woke him up and asked him to call me, it was just after 10 pm in Washington, and so it was about 3 am in the UK. I knew that God did not want me to carry on like I was, so as soon as Uncle John dropped the phone, I asked Alan to leave. He was shocked and wanted to know why, and I said, 'God will not be pleased with us if you stayed here any longer'. He felt so ashamed; I could see how red he his face was. I asked him if we could ask God for forgiveness together and also thank Him because if He hadn't asked Uncle John to call, we could have gone further in the sin of adultery. We had already sinned in our hearts and we knew it, but God, in His infinite mercies, delivered us from disaster. So we prayed together and Alan left.

"I had spent the night weeping before the Lord, I was truly repentant. I spoke to Sam about what had happened and he prayed with me. He said God had forgiven me and I must forgive myself and learn from what had happened. I didn't attend Susan's lectures for two weeks and I took some time off the internship. She didn't call to ask why I was missing and I wondered why.

"There was a knock on my door one evening; I wasn't expecting anyone, so I ignored it. The knocking carried on, and so with a little frustration, I marched over to the door and yanked it open and, much to my surprise, Susan was standing there with a bag of Chinese food in her hand and asked if she could come in. She was so nice to me that I felt like a Judas; I had betrayed her trust. She said she brought a movie and some food, and wanted us to have a girls' night in. I was so nervous, I just nodded at her. She sat beside me, really close to me and put her arm around me, she stroked my hair and said, 'Dassah, Jesus loves you and I love you too. Alan told me what happened and I have forgiven you both'. I could feel the hot tears streaming down my face. She looked right in my eyes and whilst wiping off my tears she said, 'There is temptation everywhere and the Lord commands us to flee from it, and you and Alan did just that. You must learn from this experience, it is very easy to fall into temptation and it can happen to anyone of us, we must watch and pray always and we must not be selfish, think of how your actions can affect your relationship with God, who loves you so much, and how it can affect others around you. We are all learning and we need God's strength to face and conquer our Goliaths. Mine was the fear of my husband having an affair, it has always been my fear because I know he likes women, but what I learnt from this is that it is the Lord that is the foundation and builder of my marriage, if I remain faithful to Him, He will be faithful to keep that which I hold dear. I learnt that I did not have to be afraid, because God follows Alan everywhere and He will not let Him fall. I understood this when Alan told me what had happened and I just thanked God. I wasn't afraid anymore, I knew Alan had genuinely learnt his lesson and I knew God would not let us go. Dassah, all I will say to you now is avoid all appearances of evil and the fear of the Lord will cause you to avoid evil. Watch and pray and I'm always here for you and so is Alan'.

"We watched the movie, ate and talked for a while and then she left. After Susan left, I reflected on **Romans 8: 37–39;** *yet in all these things we are more than conquerors through Him who loved us. For I am persuaded that neither death nor life, nor angels nor principalities nor powers, nor things present nor things to come, nor height nor depth, nor any other created thing, shall be able to separate us from the love of God which is in Christ Jesus our Lord (NKJV)*. I had a deeper revelation of the love of God for me, and I never wanted to sin against Him again. I prayed for Him to keep me and others in the Body of Christ from sin daily.

"My Goliath was not just David dumping me and me having to forgive him, or having to forgive myself for the sin of adultery or even accepting Susan's forgiveness. My Goliath was also not having a revelation of how much God loves me, even on the cross when Jesus was stretched out; He had me on His mind like He did that night when He asked Uncle John to phone me."

Dassah paused for a few minutes, and with a huge sigh I said to her, "You know 'many are the afflictions of the righteous but the Lord delivers him from them all' (*psalm 34:19*) and when the enemy thinks he's had us trapped, God makes a way of escape for us, if we are willing to accept a way out."

Chapter 13
Home Sweet Home

"My four years in Washington were up, I had completed my degree with Masters and I graduated top of my class. Sam had finished at MIT as well and we were heading back to England. Susan and Alan threw a 'send forth' party for us; they didn't like to say 'send off' because they believed we were heading forth into new ventures and we were still a family. Our friends from university and church were there, it was lovely. I was going to miss Alan, Susan and the kids a lot.

"We cleaned our house in Virginia and handed the keys over to the estate agent, so he could rent it out and then we were off. On the plane, I could see that Sam had a secret, he was grinning from ear to ear, and he couldn't stop smiling. I asked him what he was up to and he said 'Nothing?!', but I knew it was a lie. I was just too curious to let this go, and so I kept pressing him for answers and finally he cracked.

"He reached into his bag and brought out a little blue jewellery box, I opened it and the most beautiful diamond ring was sitting in it. 'This must have cost you a fortune,' I said.
'Yes it did, and I pray it's worth every penny.'
'Well, I know we love each other and all, but there's no way I'm wearing this ring, I mean what kind of a graduation present is this? When people ask me who I'm engaged too, I'll have to start explaining that it isn't an engagement ring, it was a....'

'Shut up D,' Sam said. 'It's not for you.'

'Oops! Oh my! You are not...! Oh don't tell me you've asked her to...' I was just so excited that I couldn't complete a whole sentence; I had so much to say as usual. 'Oh congrats Bro!'

'Thanks, but I haven't asked her yet, I'm hoping she says yes.'

'That is an expensive ring, what if she says no?'

'Well, if she's obedient to God, she won't, if she says no now, I'll wait and ask again till she says yes, because I know God gave her to me and no one else. She's the one D, and if she doesn't know that now, she will know it later; I just have to be patient. There are some things we just can't rush and this is one of them. You see, no matter what Linda says or thinks, God's word is the beginning and the end of a matter, He does not change His mind, once He has spoken His word, it is as He has spoken it. Linda is my wife and I am her husband irrespective of what we both think and feel, the only thing that can keep us apart now, is time and that too will pass.'

'Wow! Sam, that is beautiful and you know what, Linda can't turn you down, not with this beautiful thing on her finger,' I said jokingly. 'I know I won't!'

'Shut up D,' he said as he snatched the ring away from me.

'Really Sam, I'm happy for you, you deserve this. So when do you want to get married?'

'As soon as possible, I need to get a job first and my own place, then I can get married. I have an interview lined up with a construction company in Bradford and two in Oxford.'

'Oxford? Sam, that's miles away from Manchester! I always thought we'd live close to each other.'

'D, I'll always be there for you, after all we didn't go to university in the same state, but we made it through, let God's will be done, He knows what's best for us. Moreover, for all you know I may never leave Manchester.'

'I hope you're praying for me Bro, I'd like to get married too you know, now that David's out of the picture, I have no idea what to do.'

'You don't have to do anything, D, you just wait on God and He will bring your husband to you, after all He is your father and He will be the one giving you away at your wedding, so it is only right that He should be the one to approve the man for you. You'll see, He'll surprise you, just don't jump ahead of Him and be still.'

"There was something about Sam's words that brought restoration to that area of my life, I suddenly felt at peace, I knew that God would sort it out and that He didn't need my help.

"We finally arrived at Manchester, Bola and Esther were at the airport to pick us up. I was thrilled to see my baby cousin for the first time, she had grown so much and she was gorgeous. I hugged her really tightly; she reminded me of Mum, she had her eyes, same eyes as Uncle John. As soon as I saw those big, brown eyes, I knew right then that there wasn't anything I would not do to make her happy.

"It was good to be home again, especially with little Esther around now, the house was full of laughter, she was just so funny. Kids say and do the funniest and yet most amazing things.

Yewande Erinle

"Sam got a really good job in Bradford, which wasn't too far from Manchester and He and Linda had agreed to buy their house in Manchester because it would be easier for Linda to get to work. Boy! Was I thankful to God! Linda had accepted his proposal and the wedding was planned for next June, the 19th to be precise, the anniversary of Mum and Dad's passing on. It wasn't their choice actually; it was the only date the church had available. It was as if God wanted us to remember that day as a day of joy from now on, not a day of sorrow any more.

"I got a job in the hospital Uncle John worked in, it was great because I had worked there before and I knew most of the people there. This time though, I had my own office with my name above the door, how cool is that?"

Chapter 14
My Heritage

"I woke up early one morning with the words 'inheritance' and 'heritage' on my mind, I just kept hearing them over and over again and I knew that the Holy Spirit had something to say about those words, so I began to research them in the bible. I learnt a lot about God giving his people an inheritance in the Old Testament, and how He expected them to look after it. I also learnt that God maintains our inheritance if we let Him and that we have an inheritance in Christ, which comprises of an earthly inheritance and a heavenly one. I asked the Holy Spirit what the specific message for me was from this topic and what I should focus on, as this was a huge topic. I didn't get an answer at first, so I just kept studying the topic and praying concerning my inheritance.

"It was only a few months to Sam and Linda's wedding, and there was still so much to do. I was responsible of finding a venue for the reception and booking a caterer, so every day after work I would visit a few venues and meet with caterers. One afternoon I walked past a restaurant, I had never seen it before, and I knew Manchester well; this must be new I thought to myself. I walked in and I was right! It was new and there was no furniture yet. There was a lot of hammering and drilling, as the place was still under some sort of construction. I asked the builders for the owner and someone from the back shouted back 'who's asking?'

Yewande Erinle

I walked over to the counter so I could speak to him; there was just so much drilling going on in the shop that we could hardly hear each other.

"A young man came out to speak with me, he mentioned that he and his business partner had just moved here from America and had decided to open up a restaurant here. I mentioned my need for a caterer for my brother's wedding and he showed me a menu. Immediately I saw the menu, I knew straight away that this was my caterer, so I hired him on the spot. With that settled, I left for home.

"Sam and Uncle John had organised a meeting with everyone involved with the wedding two weeks before the big day. That Saturday evening, the caterer called to say that his partner would be attending the meeting, as he had to be somewhere else that day. Every one arrived at Uncle John's; there was a huge board with a checklist on it because Sam wanted to make sure that everything was covered. The meeting was due to start at six o'clock, but it was quarter past and the caterer hadn't shown up yet. Finally at about half past, the door bell rang and I opened the door, guess who was standing at the door? I could not believe my eyes, I almost passed out. It was David!

'What are you doing here?' I asked, 'I'm Steve's business partner; I own the restaurant you booked?'
'What?' I replied. *Hoooolllly Spiiirrriiiittttt? Loorrrd?! Why didn't you tell me that was David's store?* I muttered under my breath, *'Well you didn't ask!'* He said, and I could just sense His smile.

Holy Spirit Diaries

"Well, we had our meeting and I was very quiet throughout, I guess I was still in shock. Everyone else was happy to see David again and there was a lot of catching up to do. David mentioned that when he saw my name on the contract for the event, he knew he had to see me before the wedding, so he came to the meeting instead.

"I went straight to my room as soon as the meeting was over, leaving the rest of the family and David to have their fun. I certainly was not in the mood for socialising and definitely not with David, and I wondered why? I thought I had forgiven David and I was over him, *'apparently not'* the Holy Spirit said, interrupting my thoughts. *What should I do now Lord?* 'FORGIVE' He stressed, *'and let it go'*. So I got down on my knees and said, 'God, I forgive David for hurting me, I lose him and let him go, your word says that whatever I lose on earth is lost in heaven and likewise whatever I bind, so I bind the spirit of unforgiveness in my life and I in turn ask for your forgiveness Lord for having unforgiveness in my heart.'

'Well that's a lot of forgiveness in one sentence,' the Holy Spirit said jokingly, and I started laughing, I laughed so hard that I started to cry and then I cried really hard and began to pray in tongues. When it was all over, I felt so free, I had nothing against David anymore and I knew I would be comfortable around him from then on.

"As I got off my knees and sat on my bed, the Holy Spirit whispered these words, 'Now, I can give you your inheritance'.

'What are you talking about, what has my inheritance got to do with forgiving David?'

Yewande Erinle

'Wrong question,' He said. 'What you should ask is, 'what has your inheritance got to do with forgiveness?' and as soon as the Lord said that I had instant understanding. God can't bless me if I have sin lurking away somewhere in my life, but what I didn't understand was why the Lord had not revealed this sin to me ages ago. After a long conversation with the Holy Spirit in my room that night, I realised that if God had revealed it to me at the time I would not have accepted it, I would have denied the hurt and the pain and just carried on. Sometimes, it's easier to deal with these types of issues when it's thrown right in your face unsuspectingly and you know that you have no choice but to deal with it there and then. So at the time of my ignorance, while I had unforgiveness in my heart, the grace of God stepped into that area of my life. I asked the Holy Spirit what this inheritance was that He wanted to give me, and He said to wait patiently.

"I didn't get the chance to see David till the day of the wedding, and even then we were both so busy that we only had the opportunity for a quick hello. The wedding was beautiful, Sam was so blessed to have such a lovely wife and God must love Linda so much as to have blessed her with a God-fearing man like Sam. I knew Mum and Dad would be watching from heaven, and they'd be so pleased. After all, I could hear the Holy Spirit rejoicing.

"While we were clearing up, I asked the Holy Spirit to give me away at my own wedding, I told Him that I wanted Him to walk me down the aisle, and He accepted. 'When will I get married Lord, and who will it be?' He just replied, 'Be patient my dear'.

"David and I finally got some time to talk after cleaning up, he apologised for the past and I said I had already forgiven him. I told him about what happened in my room the day he came over to Uncle John's for the meeting. He told me about his life over the past four years, how he had backslid and got into a relationship with a girl who had only just given her life to Christ at the time and they both ended drawing away from God, not closer to Him. Finally he left Italy and set up a restaurant in New York, he said it was there he met Steve whom he initially hired as head chef and later made him partner. They both decided to open up a restaurant in the UK and the cheapest building they could find was here in Manchester. He had thought of contacting me over the years but didn't know what he would say to me if he did, so he just got on with his work. He spoke of how God began to teach him His word and how He sent Steve to help him find the way back to God. He invited me to visit his restaurant in New York next time I was in America, and he gave me his contact details. It was good talking to David; we laughed together and enjoyed each other's company, just like old times. He had to leave for New York the next day, he was going to spend the rest of the summer there and he asked if I'd like to come over for a few days and I said I'd think about it.

"I didn't think much of David's invitation to New York, after all we had only just met again and we were happy just being friends. David called me two or three times after he left to say hello, once he asked me if I had thought about coming over but I told him I couldn't. One morning, two months after Sam's wedding, The Lord said to me, 'I'm sending you to New York' and I asked why, but there was no answer. I got to work that day and my boss mentioned that he had booked tickets for us to attend a seminar in New York and we had to leave in two days. *Wow!* I thought to myself, *you do move quickly when you want to Lord.*

"My boss had booked us into one of the finest hotels in New York, and I was rather excited even though I had very little time to myself, as the seminar was two full days long. At the end of each day, I would just collapse on my bed and sleep till the next day. We were meant to go back to Manchester on the Friday, but my boss said I should have the weekend on him in the hotel, since I had worked so hard. I was shocked. What did I do to deserve this Lord? I asked, and again the Holy Spirit said; *'I SAID I WAS GOING TO SEND YOU TO NEW YORK, NOT YOUR BOSS BUT THIS IS ME SENDING YOU TO NEW YORK CHILD'.* There was just something about the way He said it that made me reply 'Ookayyyy Lord!'

"With a whole two days to myself, I planned to sleep, visit the spa, eat loads and sleep again; at least that was my schedule anyway. So on Saturday morning, while I was getting ready to go the spa, there was a knock on my hotel room door. Guess who it was. It was Steve."

"Wooaahh! Steve?" I interrupted. "Dassah, I guessed David and you said Steve?"

"Well you guessed wrong then. Come on Dami, thunder doesn't strike three times in the same place does it? David at my door on my 21st birthday, David at our house just before Sam's wedding, and David at my hotel room again. God's not monotonous and He's not that boring. May I proceed?"

"Well! I was expecting David, but carry on…"

"Anyway, Steve said that David asked him to pick me up and bring me to the restaurant. I wondered how he knew I was in town; after all I hadn't contacted him. Steve later mentioned that Uncle John had phoned to let David know where I was so he could keep me company. *'Well thanks Uncle John'*, I thought. I reluctantly went with Steve, it was a little over 45-minutes drive, and when I got to the restaurant, I had the shock of my life. The restaurant's name was Hadassah! I could not feel my legs, I needed help getting out of the car, I mean this place was over three years old, and you mean David still thought of me? He named the place after me, or is there another Hadassah? I recovered quickly and walked right in. David met us at the door, we hugged and he took me round the place. I just had to ask why he named his restaurant Hadassah?

'Well, God asked me to,' he said. 'And you've got to admit, it's a beautiful name, even for a restaurant.' Then I did the most embarrassing thing; I wept, and David wiped my tears. Immediately I heard the words 'your inheritance'.

"We had dinner at Hadassah's and I stayed behind to help Steve and David close up, I guess God had another schedule for me and mine just went out the window. I thought that was my best night in such a long time, I was amongst friends and I had eaten a fine meal in a very posh restaurant named after me, what more could I ask for? And, just as I had finished thinking that, David mentioned that he had forgotten the dessert and that I had to try it. I was already too full, but I didn't want to be rude, so I agreed; as soon as I said yes, Steve decided it was time for him to go.

'What? You're not having dessert?' I asked.

'No thanks,' he said. 'I've got to go now, see you some other time.'

Yewande Erinle

"David asked me to sit at the bar, and wait for him to get the dessert ready. When he left for the kitchen, I heard the word 'inheritance' again, and I said, Lord, I get it. The restaurant was named after me and the Lord laughed. I found myself thinking of how mature David was now, how he had changed and how sweet and charming he was.

"Finally David came out with a huge bowl of chocolate and vanilla sundae, decorated with Mars bars, the British ones (my favourite chocolate I might add) and strawberries, and right in the middle on the top of this magnificent sundae, was a good-sized diamond. I thought, how odd, a diamond on a sundae.

'This must be an expensive sundae,' I said jokingly and David replied, 'You don't know the half of it, take it out so we can enjoy our dessert.' So I did just that, I took out the diamond, and to my surprise, it wasn't just a diamond, it was the most beautiful ring I had ever seen, even more beautiful than Linda's one. I placed my hand over my mouth in shock, I was speechless. David took my hand in his and said, 'I know you have every reason to say no, but I know that God made me for you and you for me, and I knew this day would come, I prayed earnestly that God would put the right words in my mouth so that I do not lose my inheritance.' As soon as I heard that word, 'inheritance', tears flooded my eyes and I just found myself nodding.

'Is that a yes he asked?'

'Yes!' I screamed, he was so excited that he grabbed me in his arms and started to shout thanks to God.

"When the excitement was over, we had dessert and I couldn't wait to get back to my hotel so I could call everyone back home and give them the good news, even though I knew they would be fast asleep, but that was no problem for me at all. That night, after David dropped me off, I got another revelation of the topic 'inheritance'. You see, the Holy Spirit is the administrator of our wealth or inheritance, and when we are mature enough, to handle the responsibilities that come with our inheritance or heritage, He hands it over to us, little by little of course. Not only did God give me a string of restaurants in my name, He gave me a man of my own and He handed me all these things when He knew I was ready to have them and look after them properly.

"David took me to the airport on Sunday evening; we decided that we would get married next April, here in New York. We felt that it was only fitting that Hadassah be the venue for our reception. I asked David how he was so sure I would say yes, why he risked naming the restaurant Hadassah and buying such an expensive ring.

'The answer is simple,' he said. 'When God tells you to do something, you just have to do it, trusting that He has your best interests at heart and that He will be glorified, whether you like the outcome or not. So, in this case, I put my feelings for you and my fear of possible rejection aside and I made it all about obeying God. I put Him first and did not worry too much about the outcome, although I was a little bit scared, I didn't want you to reject me, but I wanted to please God much more than I feared you rejecting me.'

'How enlightening,' I thought."

Chapter 15
Bone of my bone, Flesh of my Flesh

"April came really fast, David and I got married in New York and had decided to live in London, a new Hadassah was opening up there. Steve was managing the one in Manchester, and David had hired someone to manage the one in New York. We decided to manage the one in London ourselves."

"Okay, stop now," I said as I ran out to check the name of the breakfast shop I was in, yep it was called Hadassah alright.

"I can see that you're catching on really quickly...Right, so we decided to make this Hadassah a little different to the others. Down here is the breakfast shop, and upstairs is the diner."

"So you gave up your job to be a waitress?"

"No, I work in a hospital here in London and, on my days off, I come in to help my husband."

"David is here?"

"Well, he is the chef here and he does own the place, I would hope that he is here."

"Do I detect a little sarcasm?"

"Only joking. HONNEEYYY! Come out and meet our new friend, she's the writer, you know, the one H.S. said was coming to see us today."

"Woah! Wait one minute, you call Him H.S. too? That's what I.... Wait a minute, what did you mean by the one whom

H.S. said was coming...? Did He tell you I was coming here? You mean He set this whole thing up? But why?"

David appeared from the kitchen. "Hello, nice to meet you, hope we managed to get rid of those hunger pangs and we won't be attacked by whatever was in there."

"Oh how embarrassing, you heard my hunger pangs?"

"No, he didn't. I told him what you said and he said, she's the one, H.S. said she was funny and always in a hurry."

"He does know me well. But why did he set up this meeting?"

"Well that we can't tell you, we can only tell you that He wanted you to hear this story. You'll have to ask Him why?" David replied.

"So Dassah, you still haven't said why you don't have a gospel music career."

"Aaah! I almost forgot. You see, when I asked H.S. to give me away at my wedding, I also made a vow that if He were to bless me with the most amazing man, filled with the Holy Ghost and led by Him, then I would give Him my voice. I would sing for charities, events and so on, but never collect a dime. God was very quick to respond to my vow. I have David and now I get invited to places to sing His praises."

"This is some testimony, the world has to hear it and learn about the goodness of our Father."

Just as I said that, both David and Dassah started laughing.

"Why are you laughing? Did I say something funny?"

"No!" David said. "It's not you, it's H.S. He's done it again. You know, He makes you answer your own question sometimes?"

"You've lost me."

"Well, you wanted to know why He set this whole thing up. He just gave you the answer, 'the world needs to hear of His goodness' and who better to tell the world than you, His writer."

"Wow! One last question Dassah, how was your wedding?"

"Well we got married three months ago and the wedding was beautiful. Guess who gave me away? Yes! The Holy Spirit, I felt Him walk down that aisle with me. He said He was very proud to be giving His daughter away to His wonderful son. He asked me to take good care of Him or I'd have to answer to Him. People said our vows were the most beautiful words they had ever heard at a wedding."

"And your first kiss?"

"Now! That was worth waiting for. It was wonderful, I thought I could hear angels singing. David's kiss was like honey on my lips and I didn't want him to stop, but we had an audience so of course we had to stop. Now I demand to wake up to his kisses."

"You know I've got to ask for those vows right?"

Chapter 16
The Vows

David's vows:

"Hadassah, my Queen, I bless the Lord for creating you especially for me. I know He had me in mind when He made you, because He placed all those qualities that I desire in you. "He gave you these big beautiful eyes just for me, so each time I look in them, I see Him and fall in love with you all over again, with those eyes you have stolen my heart forever. He gave you these beautiful, slender yet strong arms, so whenever you hold me, I feel His presence and so I only ever long for your arms and no one else's. When I lay my head on your chest, it's just like heaven, there's just so much peace when I hear His heart beat through yours and then I realise that mine beats to the same rhythm.

"I love you my darling, you are much more beautiful than tens of thousands of women and today I vow to love you, submit to you and protect you with my life. I pray for you more than I pray for myself and when challenges come our way, I will rely entirely on His wisdom and love to see us through.

"May God fill me always to overflowing with love for you till He calls us home and may He be a cord around us, getting tighter and tighter every single day. No weapon fashioned against this love will prosper because God is the founder and builder of this city."

Yewande Erinle

Hadassah's vows:

"David my King, I love you. God has placed you as a crown over my head. You are my glory and I will love, honour and obey you always. "My husband and my King, I kneel before God almighty and before you, thanking Him for giving you to me. Now I know without a shadow of a doubt that I'm always on His mind because He gave me a provider, a lover, a friend, a shield and a warrior all in one package. "Your kisses to me are sweeter than wine and the sound of your name is music to my ears. Your name is like perfume poured out. I long for your touch always and there is much safety in your arms. God has blessed you with the strength of ten thousand men, you are my Boaz and I trust God in you to keep our love safe.

"My King, our love is God, so it will last forever because God cannot die and so neither will our love. Together we will walk in His love and fulfil divine destiny. We will feel no evil as long as we obey His word together and put Him first.

"David, my love, my heart will long for you always and these arms will be there to bring you comfort in tough times and my mouth will speak words of wisdom for direction when you need it. I will pour praises on you like oil and my kisses on you like perfume. With my body I will honour you and today the Lord has bound us together as one and nothing will tear us apart in Jesus' name.

"I could go on forever, but then we will have to spend our honeymoon here (which I look forward to by the way). God has kept me for you and today He is presenting me to you as a gift.

A gift that you will unwrap with your own hands and delight in always. It is my desire to please you always till we go and reign with Him in eternity. I love you my King."

"That is beautiful, what did the priest say after that? I'm guessing he didn't have to say much!"

"You are right actually; he closed his bible and said 'Need I say more, you may kiss the bride', replied David.

"It was my first proper kiss and it was worth waiting for, I didn't want it to end and I still never want it to end," Dassah added.

"And it never will sweetheart,' David said, gazing into Dassah's eyes lovingly, he leaned over and gently kissed her.

Notes

Dassah's story is such a beautiful one that I had to share it with the world. Even though she had been through a lot of disappointment and hurt, she remained constant in her walk with God, waiting on Him diligently and expecting that He will come through for her always. Well He did and still does. He blessed her with a man that most women wish for and He has been their guide, teacher and comforter through the years and no doubt He always will be.

God did not just give Dassah a Godly man for a husband; He blessed her with both spiritual and physical wealth. Her intimate relationship with God gave her the gift of prophecy that enabled her to pray the right prayers for her aunt in the hospital. God taught her the importance of forgiveness, which is something we all need to learn, as it is vital to our spiritual and physical growth. Unforgiveness is a sin and it prevents us from walking closely with God, it is a cancer of the spirit and it must be cut out. Dassah's and Sam's school fees were paid with part of their inheritance money (from their parents), so they were not in debt when they graduated from university. Dassah now had three restaurants in her name, was a qualified psychologist and counsellor, and she raised funds for well-known charities by singing gospel songs.

Yewande Erinle

Dassah's life is not without challenges, though her marriage is still very new and they are in love with each other, they will face new mountains that they have to either move or climb together. But you know, with their track record and with what God has placed on the inside of them, they will overcome these challenges and that is worth looking forward to, the victory at the end of a battle, the victory that Jesus promised us.

From this story, I learnt that it is worth waiting on God for all of our needs. It is worth obeying Him and working in His will. Hadassah, kept herself pure till the day God decided to give her away to David and that is such a beautiful thing. Yes, she had challenges and it was by no means easy, but she loved the Lord and was passionate about Him, and it is that passion, that zeal, that performed all God's work in her life.

The world we live in today is full of challenges for us all, especially for the children of God, but take one day at a time, trust in the Lord that if you fall He will pick you up and dust you off again, and put you back on the right track. Take each day at a time; He's got His eyes on you.

Hadassah's relationship with the Holy Spirit is one to be desired and I know it may sound impossible to a lot of Christians, but I urge you to give it a try today. Ask the Holy Spirit to be your best friend, your guide, teacher and comforter, tell Him you cannot make a move without His voice, ask Him to make you long for Him day and night and help you recognise Him when He does come. After all, it is His desire to tabernacle with and in you.

If you have just read this book and you don't even know what it is to have God as your father or Jesus as your saviour and you'd like this, can I first direct you to the book of John in the Bible, chapter 3 verse 16; *'For God so loved the world, that he gave his only begotten Son, that whosoever believeth in him should not perish, but have everlasting life'* (KJV). You see, Jesus had to die for us all, so that we can have this beautiful relationship with God. Jesus rose again on the third day, he defeated His enemy and ours, the Devil, so that we can be free to spend our days on earth with God and experience the fullness of His joy, peace, love and righteousness.

You know what? Just ask the Lord to forgive you for all your sins, because all of us have sinned whether we know it or not and whether we agree or not, but His word says we have all sinned and His son had to shed His blood to wash away our sins. He shed all that blood on the cross of Calvary so that we never have to live in sin or be bound by it again. So ask Him to forgive you and come into your life as your Lord and Saviour. You might wonder why you have to say it, well the answer is simple, because the word of God asks you to believe with your heart that Jesus died for you – confesses it with your mouth and you will be saved (**Romans 10:10** *'For with the heart man believeth unto righteousness; and with the mouth confession is made unto salvation').* It requires obedience and faith, the latter develops daily, so don't worry, just start with obeying His word just like you saw the characters in this book do.

We heard Dassah and David say their vows to each other didn't we? Well, it's a bit like that, telling the Lord that you love Him and want Him in your life as your King forever! Give it a go; I promise that your life will never be the same, as long as you are willing to obey His word. Spend more time studying the word of God; it's His way of introducing Himself to you.

A Letter from 'The Father' to His Daughter

My darling daughter,

I made you with my own hands, you are beautiful and I love you. I loved you in the past, I love you now and I will always love you. It doesn't matter what you have done or what you have been through, all that matters is that you experience this love that I have for you. This love I have for you will heal you, it will guide and protect you, and it will direct you and keep you safe forever.

My arms are open wide, run into them. I long to hold you tight in my arms, you cannot run deep enough into them, there is still so much depth in me for you to reach, my love has no end and it has no limits.

My love will take you from the pits of hell and death to the gates of Zion and into my presence. My love will promote you into greatness to which I have called you. My love will cause you to laugh again, to know joy, to have fun, to love again and live abundantly.

My princess, I love you and want you. I've got so much more in store for you, just come, come darling, come and get it.

Yewande Erinle

Let go and let love. My love is able to see you through all of life's hardships; it will wipe the tears from your eyes. You will never know loneliness when you are with me. I will never disappoint you, I will never leave you or forsake you, I will never abuse you or your trust, and I will never betray you.

Come! Trust me; let's walk together. I can fill the void inside, and my word will make you whole. Take my hand and follow me, you are priceless to me, much more precious than gold and more beautiful than the purest diamond.

I love you.

Abba Father.

Reference

Except otherwise stated, all scripture references are taken from The Holy Bible, New King James Version (NKJV)

About the author

Yewande Erinle is a pharmacovigilance project manager. She is married to Lanre Erinle and they have three children. Yewande completed her first degree in Pharmacology, at the University of Portsmouth, UK and then went on to complete a masters degree in immunology at Imperial college London, UK.

Yewande works in the youth ministry in her home church and currently runs a bible club at her children's school.

Printed in Great Britain
by Amazon.co.uk, Ltd.,
Marston Gate.